JIU JITSU IN WWII
DUTCH RESISTANCE FIGHTERS
AND SECRET AGENTS

THE JIU JITSU PHOTO ALBUM OF
HANS VAN DER STOK

-Second edition-

ISBN 978-90-8666-431-3

JIU JITSU IN WWII
DUTCH RESISTANCE FIGHTERS
AND SECRET AGENTS

THE JIU JITSU PHOTO ALBUM OF
HANS VAN DER STOK

Compiled by J.H.G Smits

-Second edition-

Contents

Preface

For more than a decade I have been researching the history of jiu jitsu in the Netherlands from 1900 to 1945, and I have always had a particular interest in the Second World War years. Owing perhaps to a prevailing sense of peril and uncertainty, jiu jitsu became increasingly popular in the Netherlands during those dark days.

While researching another book, I stumbled upon a photo album which had been a gift to a well-known Dutch jiu jitsu master, Johan van der Bruggen. In the war years, Van der Bruggen was also the only teacher of judo in the Netherlands.

The album had belonged to one of his jiu jitsu students, Hans van der Stok, and it contains a note that Van der Stok died in captivity in 1945 in Mauthausen concentration camp. Further research revealed that Hans, an ardent practitioner of jiu jitsu, had escaped from occupied Holland to England, trained as a secret service agent and returned to Holland to join the Dutch resistance. While resisting the occupation of his homeland he was captured, imprisoned and eventually executed.

Reflecting on this I was deeply moved. At first I planned to devote a chapter of my history of jiu jitsu in the Netherlands to Hans van der Stok. Eventually, I decided to publish the photo album in its entirety to give present-day practitioners and other readers the chance to get acquainted with this remarkable young man.

This publication is the result of that decision.

Thanks to its unique photographic material, this album gives us a clearer picture of the history of jiu jitsu in the Netherlands. Although it is intended primarily as a tribute to Hans van der Stok, I felt that the album's historical importance gave me licence to add my own explanatory notes to the photographs. In the original album the photographs appeared without commentary.

For this publication I have maintained the order of the photographs as they appeared in the original album. However, I have taken the liberty of enlarging certain photos, and in some cases I have dedicated a full page to a single photo while the original album featured two or even four photos to a page.

Hans van der Stok's story fully deserves to be told and I hope this publication will give him some of the recognition he deserves.

J.H.G. Smits
Zoetermeer, 4 January 2011

Preface to the second edition

Since the first publication of the Jiu Jitsu Photo Album of Hans van der Stok, I have been researching the role of jiu jitsu and its practitioners in the Dutch resistance during the Second World War. This expanded second edition of the photo album contains the results of that research. A further volume on several other Dutch practitioners of jiu jitsu who were involved in resistance activities during the War will be published in the near future.

Jiu jitsu in The Netherlands

At the start of the 20th century, the practice of jiu jitsu spread from Japan to Europe. In the United Kingdom, France and Germany it was taught by a select number of practitioners.

Jiu jitsu was introduced in the Netherlands by P.M.C. Toepoel, a boxing and PE instructor with a keen interest in self-defence. He had learned some jiu jitsu in Paris and London from Japanese teachers residing there. Between 1910 and 1918, he started teaching jiu jitsu in The Hague, and from there the art began to gradually spread. In the subsequent decades, a number of instructors emerged in the Netherlands, such as K.T. Yo, L. Boretius, V. Kasulakow, Maurice van Nieuwenhuizen, A.W.Tops and Johan van der Bruggen.

Prior to 1940, there were probably no more than ten jiu jitsu instructors working in the Netherlands, and there was no cooperation to speak of between them. It was probably Van Nieuwenhuizen who conceived the idea for a jiu jitsu association, possibly as early as 1937 or 1938. The organization in question became the Nederlandsche Jiu Jitsu Bond (NJJB), and was quickly regarded as the official body for the art in the Netherlands. The NJJB offered courses for an officially recognized instructor's certificate while students could train for an amateur certificate. At first only one amateur certificate was available, though later practitioners could obtain amateur certificates A, B and C.

Johan van der Bruggen

Johan van der Bruggen was born in 1916 in Haarlem. When he was three years old his family travelled to the Dutch East Indies (now Indonesia), settling in Surabaya. At thirteen, Johan was introduced to jiu jitsu and judo by a Japanese resident named Taiji Nakada.

Johan trained daily until 1935, the year he received a Japanese certificate of mastery from Nakada. The same year, he returned to the Netherlands to further his education.

Johan van der Bruggen, 1940

It is unclear what made him change his plans, but not long after arriving in the Netherlands Johan started teaching jiu jitsu. He offered lessons in a small backroom of the chess club 'De Westertoren' in Rotterdam. After teaching in various locations in the city, he opened the First Rotterdam Jiu Jitsu and Judo School in 1938.

Van der Bruggen's no-nonsense approach, both in training and teaching, suited the down-to-earth people of Rotterdam. His lessons quickly grew popular and his school flourished. All was well until early May 1940, when most of the city centre was destroyed by the German air force in the bombing of Rotterdam. Van der Bruggen's *dojo* was completely destroyed.

The bombing of Rotterdam. Images of a scrapbook
from Johan van der Bruggen, may 1940

Van Nieuwenhuizen ran a sport school in The Hague where he taught jiu jitsu. After Van der Bruggen's *dojo* was destroyed, he started teaching at Van Nieuwenhuizen's school until he got an opportunity to open a school of his own again. In September 1941 he opened the 'Nakada' school in The Hague's Zoutmanstraat.

I have been unable to discover when or where Hans van der Stok first began to train in jiu jitsu, but eventually he became a student of Johan van der Bruggen. Research on Van der Bruggen's role in the Dutch resistance is still ongoing. Although it is not yet clear whether he himself was a member, what is certain is that he taught jiu jitsu to several people who were actively involved in the resistance.

Biographical sketch

Johan Paul ('Hans') van der Stok was born in Balikpapan, Borneo in the Dutch East Indies on 21 March 1919. He was the son of Cornelis van der Stok and Annie van der Stok-Snetlaghe. He had two brothers, Felix and Bram, and a sister, Anke.

Hans joined the navy as a cadet at the age of 20 and was placed at the Royal Naval College. By May 1940, he held the rank of cadet corporal, serving on HNLMS *Hertog Hendrik*. A month later he was serving on HNLMS *Buffel*. On 15 July the same year he was honourably discharged when his job was abolished under the German occupation.

Hans seized on the idea of escaping to England after the successful escape of his older brother, flight officer Bram (Bob) van der Stok, together with Peter Tazelaar and Erik Hazelhoff Roelfzema, in July 1941.

In June 1942 Hans signed on with a ship sailing from Delfzijl to Sweden, where he reported to the Royal Dutch Embassy in Stockholm.

On 22 February 1943 he arrived in Scotland and took up active duty once more. A week later he reached England and was assigned to the Dutch Special Operations Bureau (Bureau Bijzondere Opdrachten) with the navy rank of cadet corporal.

He carried with him a message for the Dutch government-in-exile in London from Henk Deinum.[1] Deinum and Marinus Vader, a friend of Hans', believed that a radio-telegraph link between occupied Holland and the Dutch government in London would be a vital communication channel. The message contained a proposal and plans for establishing the link.

Once in London, Hans approached the Bureau Inlichtingen, the Dutch government's intelligence service, where he was employed as a radio operator.

The Bureau had been founded to create and maintain a regular connection between the government-in-exile and the Dutch resistance. It worked closely with the British Secret Intelligence Service (SIS).

Later, Hans trained as an agent with the Bureau. He was schooled in encrypting and decoding messages, unarmed combat (in which his training in jiu jitsu must have been useful), firearms, parachuting and riding a motorcycle. He also received special training in microphotography from the British SIS.

On the night of 19 September 1943, Hans parachuted into occupied Holland together with fellow agent Otto Martin Wiedemann. They landed safely close to Middenmeer.

The agents' brief was to contact Louis 'd Aulnis,[2] Fiat Libertas[3] and the radio service of the Raad van het Verzet (Council of Resistance).[4] Expanding the reach of the Council's transmissions was considered vital as this would greatly enlarge the Bureau's sphere of operations.

Upon landing, Hans took refuge at the home of his brother Felix on the Prinsengracht in Amsterdam. At several addresses in Amsterdam he established radio contact between the Ordedienst,[5] the Bureau Inlichtingen and the Dutch government-in-exile.

As well as his duties as an agent Hans also served as a radio telegrapher, code breaker and micro-photographer for the Zendgroep Barbara[6] and provided support to the Groep Packard.[7]

During radio transmissions to the Bureau he used the code names 'Hans' and 'Johansen'. His alias 'in the field' was Jan de Vries.

Through Chris Tonnet, his contact in the Ordedienst, Hans obtained a house in the Courbetstraat in Amsterdam to use as a base for his activities, including developing photographic materials. Fellow agent Reijer Abraham Grisnigt worked with Hans from this address. Grisnigt sent his messages for the Bureau and the government-in-exile from the Prinsengracht address, the house belonging to Hans' brother Felix.

On 2 February 1944 Bram Grisnigt, Hans and Felix were arrested after the German security service triangulated their radio signal.

Hans van der Stok was transported to Mauthausen where he was executed on 11 April 1945.

Hans was posthumously awarded the Bronze Cross by Royal Decree no. 26, dated 6 June 1956:

'Through his courage in the face of the enemy has distinguished himself as an agent of the secret intelligence service. Sent into occupied territory, he performed a perilous task in extremely difficult conditions, which after an enemy counter operation led ultimately to his death.'

Hans was described by friends and colleagues as a genial, good-natured and level-headed young man.

Bram Grisnigt's reminiscences

In early January 1943, two men met in London beneath the great clock at Victoria Railway Station. Hans van der Stok introduced himself as 'Johansen' and Bram Grinsnigt gave his name as 'Kees Coster'.

Hans and Bram were part of a group of ten aspiring intelligence agents. They were to report to a liaison officer of the British Secret Intelligence Service, who would accompany them to a training centre, a villa known as 'Huize Anna' in West Dulwich, south London.

This was the first group of agents of the newly formed Dutch intelligence service, the Bureau Inlichtingen. For security reasons all agents used an alias. They were also prohibited from visiting clubs and public places, such as 'Oranje Haven', that were frequented by Dutch exiles.

Hans and Symen Verhagen trained as micro-photographers while other agents trained in radiotelegraphy and cryptography. All training was facilitated by the British. Hans and Bram travelled daily from West Dulwich into central London by train.

The agents' basic training consisted of a parachute course at Ringway Airport (now Manchester Airport), close combat (dirty fighting, disabling opponents), shooting, motorcycle riding, swimming and running. Hans was an accomplished sportsman and an excellent swimmer.

Hans and Bram got along well – they would dine together from time to time at a Chinese restaurant in Piccadilly – but, like the other agents, they generally kept themselves to themselves when not on duty.

On the night of 19 September 1943, Bram and fellow agent Piet Hoekman were dropped near Beugen, a village in the Dutch province of Noord Brabant. They should have been dropped in the vicinity of Escharen but due to a navigation error they landed about 15 kilometres to the south.

All agents of the Bureau Inlichtingen were dropped 'blind', meaning there was no liaison waiting to assist them on the ground.
After landing in a farmyard, Bram and Piet heard men's voices in the dark. They drew their pistols but encountered no one, and fortunately the night passed without incident. The next morning they set off towards their contact address in Escharen.

The same night Hans and an agent called Wiedemann were parachuted into Noord Holland province. Hans and Bram later met up in Amsterdam. Hans' alias was now 'De Vries', while Bram's was 'Poot'. Working together with Henk Letteboer, another radio telegraphist from the Bureau Inlichtingen, Bram and Hans divided the workload and got on with the business of encrypting and decoding messages.

Bram slept usually in a house on the Nieuw Looisterstraat and transmitted his messages from houses at 485 and 1047 Prinsengracht. These properties were rented by Hans' brother, reserve officer Felix van der Stok. Bram would sometimes send messages from an attic room at the address where Hans was living, on the Coubetstraat. This was the address where Hans stored his photographic equipment.

On Wednesday 2 February 1944, while Bram was transmitting messages from the attic at 1047 Prinsengracht, he heard someone coming up the stairs. Assuming it was Hans, he continued transmitting. The next moment he was overrun by agents of the German Sicherheitsdienst, or SD (the intelligence branch of the SS).

The Germans – a group numbering 36 men – had already found their way onto the roof and searched the rest of the house. After being marched downstairs to the living room, Bram tried to fight off his captors and make a run for it, but he was quickly subdued and beaten about the face. Moments later, Hans arrived with a stovepipe under his arm. Discovering the Germans, he claimed he had come from the forge to deliver the stovepipe, but since he'd entered the house with a key the Germans did not believe him. No sooner had they arrested Hans than his brother Felix arrived. On searching him, the SD agents found a pistol and ammunition. All three Dutch agents were taken to the notorious SD police station at Euterpestraat. This was the last that Bram ever saw of Hans and Felix.

Bram Grisnigt speaking in 2016:
'Hans and I got along very well, although we never had particularly deep conversations. He was an excellent sportsman. The fact that Hans and Felix were arrested and died in a concentration camp because of my radio transmissions has always been a source of great sorrow to me.'

The photo album

Although Hans' album is a scrap book and photo album, it is
compiled in such a way that it may have doubled as a simple
handbook for jiu jitsu techniques. This seems likely, as Hans started
the album in August 1940, at a time when no good illustrated book
on jiu jitsu existed in the Netherlands.

The Nederlandse Jiu Jitsu Bond or NJJB, an association of Dutch jiu
jitsu instructors, was founded in 1939 by Maurice van Nieuwenhuizen
and Johan van der Bruggen. The organisation issued the A, B and C
amateur certificates and an instructor's licence.

This photo album features most of the techniques students had to
master to obtain the 'C' amateur certificate.

Photographs 1 to 31 were taken at Van Nieuwenhuizen's sport school
at 384 Laan van Meerdervoort in The Hague. Photographs 33 to 41
and 43 to 46 were shot at the Haagse Jiu Jitsu School (later the
Nakada school), Van der Bruggen's school at 61a Zoutmanstraat in
The Hague.

Photographs 47 to 64 were taken during a demonstration by Johan
van der Bruggen and his students at the Pulchri Studio in The Hague.

Where possible I have given the names of the techniques shown in
the photographs. In the early days of jiu jitsu in the Netherlands, the
Japanese names of techniques were not commonly used, though Van
der Bruggen did refer to them occasionally. I have used the names
under which the techniques were known at that time.

Where possible, I have identified the names of the individuals and
locations featured in the photographs.

Hans, August 1940, The Hague

Presented to Johan van der Bruggen in remembrance of Cadet Sergeant
Hans van der Stok,
who passed away in Mauthausen on 11 April 1945.

A. Van der Stok-Snetlaghe

Photos 1 and 2: Interior of the sport school run by Maurice van Nieuwenhuizen, who is standing far left in the second photo. Van der Bruggen executes a kidney scissor while lying on his back. Hans van der Stok (dressed all in white) is on tiptoe in the first photo (while being held in an arm lock). The photos show two different arm locks (a bent-arm lock and an arm lock from the side).

Photo 3: Van Nieuwenhuizen executes a combination arm lock-strangle on Van der Bruggen.

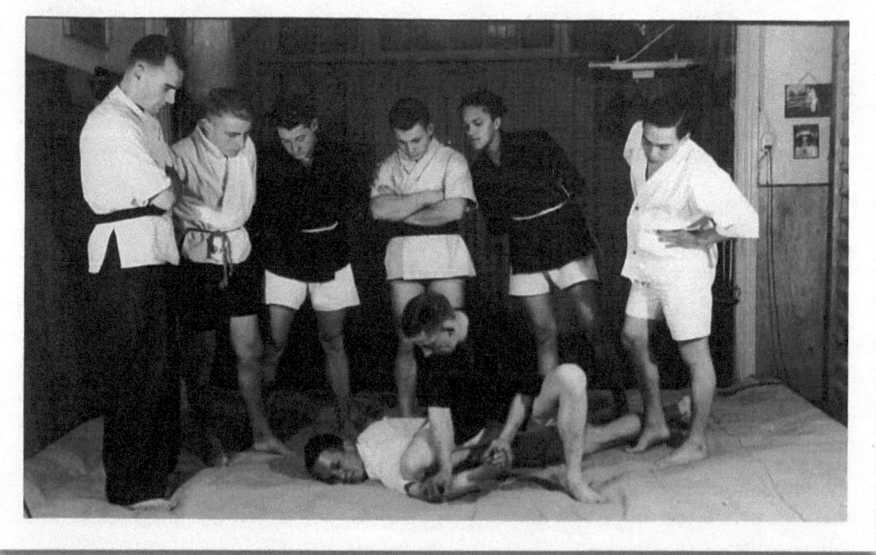

Photo 4: Arm lock with knee on the upper arm.

Photos 5 and 6: Maurice van Nieuwenhuizen breaking his fall.

23

Photo 7: Maurice van Nieuwenhuizen shows the right way to break your fall sideways on.

Photo 8: A push to the chin, pressure on the nerves in the neck, as defence from a body clasp.

Photos 9 and 10: Beginning and end of a bent-arm lock.

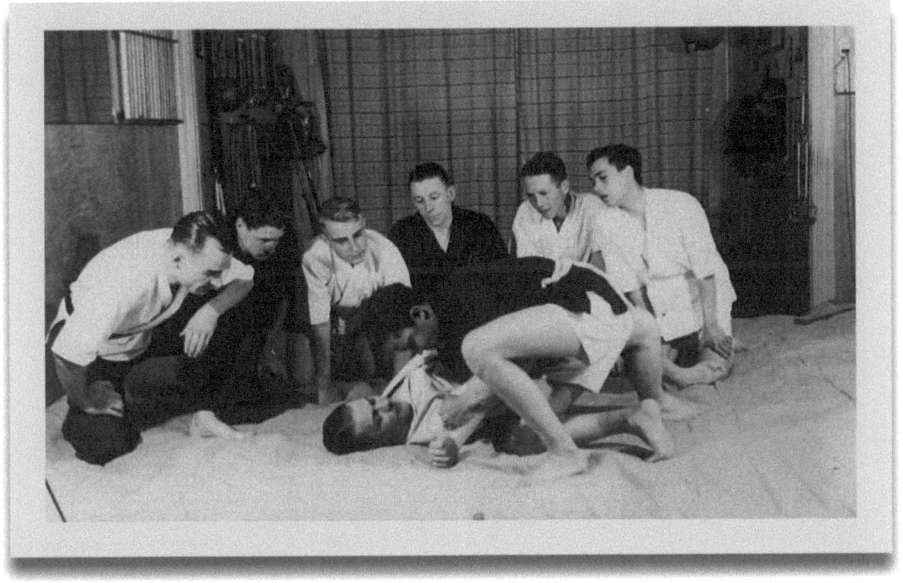

Photo 11: Ankle turn as defence to a kick.

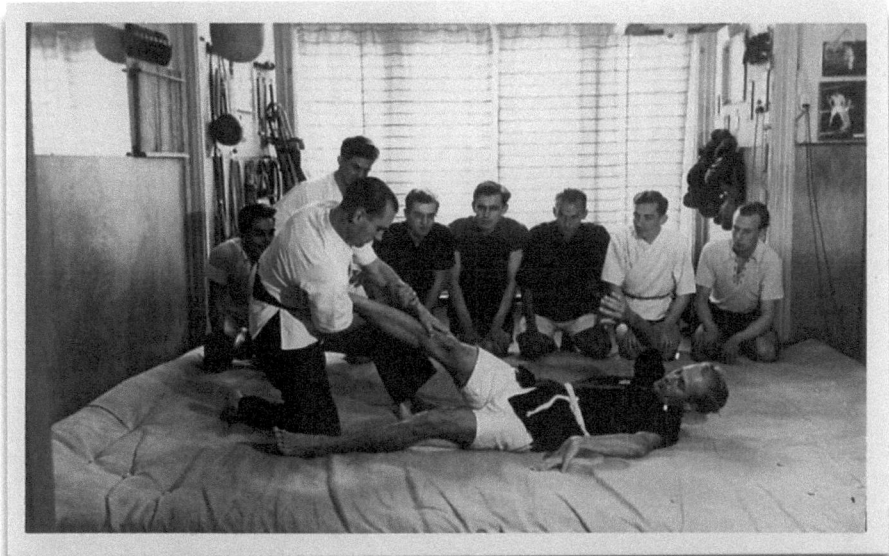

Photos 12 and 13: Alternative defence against kick: photo 12 shows the end situation, while photo 13 shows the initial capture of the leg. It is possible that the order of photos was changed at some point. NB. it is also possible to lock the leg after turning the ankle.

At this time the technical curriculum as taught by the Dutch jiu jitsu association, the NJJB, included two defences against kicking attacks.

Photo 14: Van Nieuwenhuizen demonstrates a stomach throw on Van der Bruggen.

Photo 15: The same stomach throw a split-second later.

Photo 16: Shoulder throw performed on Van Nieuwenhuizen.

Photo 17: Shoulder throw performed by the instructors.

Photo 18: A clasp around the arms from behind. The defence is a throw executed by bending the body and pushing both knees.

Photo 19: The same technique.

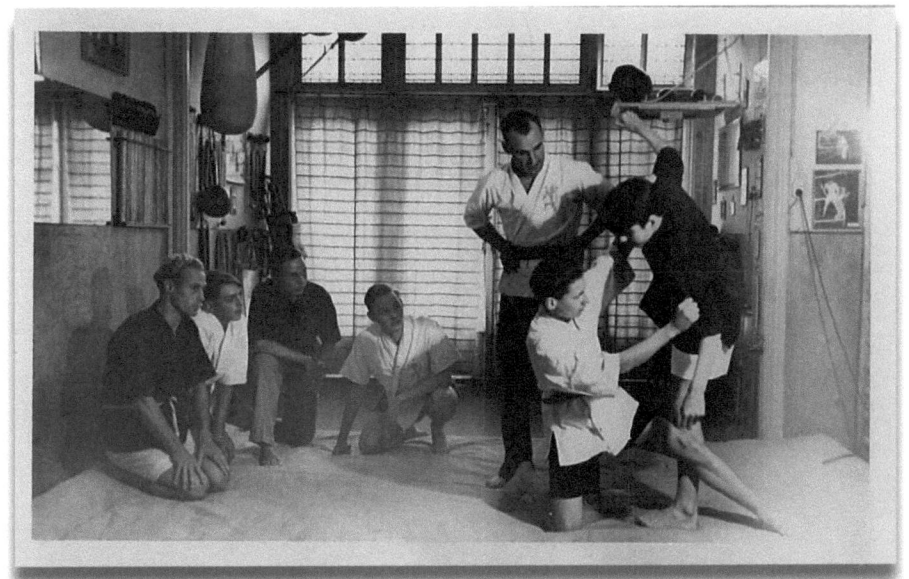

Photo 20: Stretched-out knee roll.

Photo 21: Van der Bruggen demonstrates the shoulder wheel.

Photo 22: Flying hip throw (or hip sway) as defence against right hook. Note that breaking your fall when using this technique is difficult and not without risk.

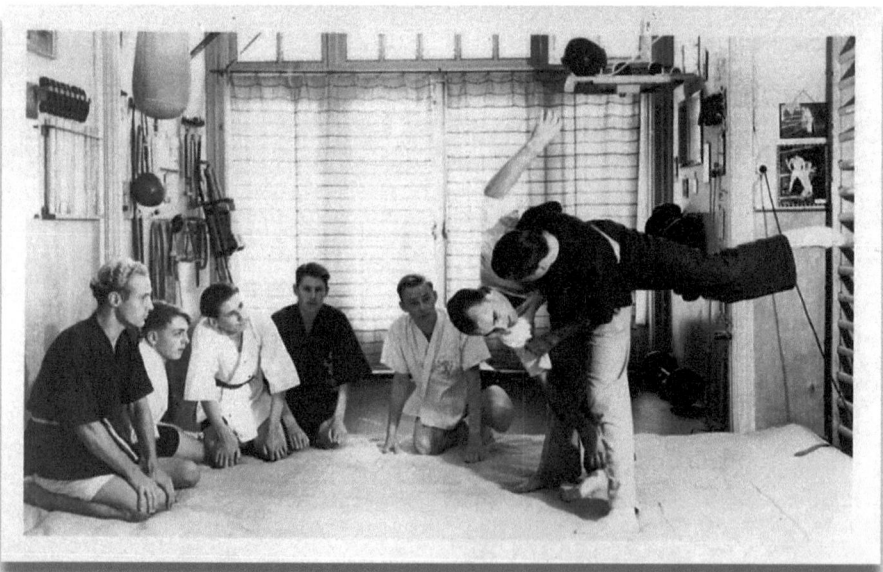

Photo 23: Hip throw performed on Van Nieuwenhuizen.

Photo 24: First hip throw (or backward hip throw). At this time there were four hip throws taught in jiu jitsu: the 1ˢᵗ, 2ⁿᵈ and 3ʳᵈ and the flying hip throw.

Photo 25: Outside ankle sweep, in which the defender uses the outside of the foot to sweep away the outside of the assailant's foot.

Photo 26: Van Nieuwenhuizen demonstrates a flying kick. This technique was not required for the amateur certificate C.

Photo 27: Van Nieuwenhuizen demonstrates an arm throw.

Photo 28: Defence against a double Nelson.

Photos 29 and 30: Two stages of a chin throw against a straight punch.

Photo 31: Reverse outside wrist lock.

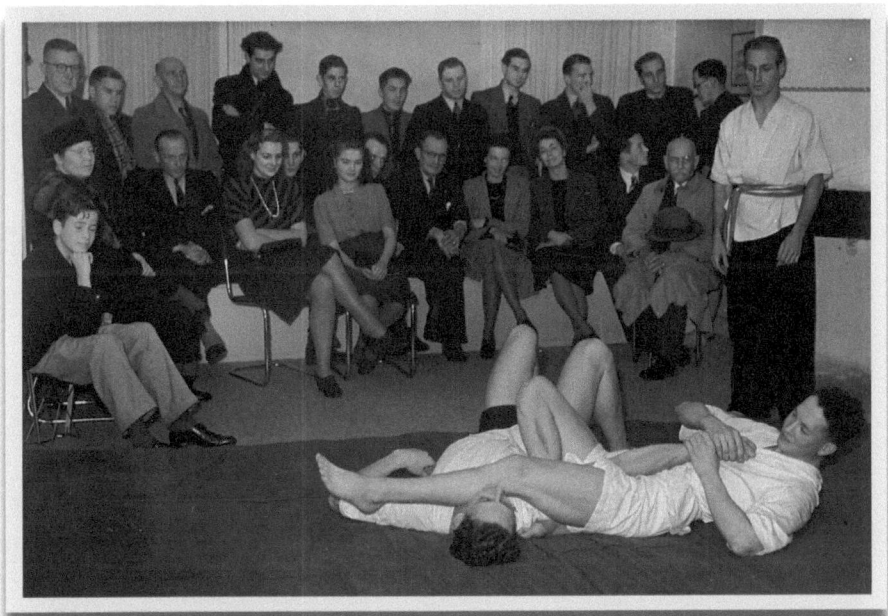

Photo 32: During a demonstration, Hans van der Stok performs a straight-arm lock while Johan van der Bruggen looks on.

Photo 33: Group photo at Van der Bruggen's school at Zoutmanstraat 61a, The Hague.

Back row, left to right: unidentified; unidentified; A. Dullaart; unidentified; Johan van der Bruggen.
Front-row, left to right: Mr Wijnberg; L. Frank; Hans van der Stok; Hans v/d Velde (assistant instructor).

Photos 34, 35 and 36: The stages, shown in order, of the double stomach throw.

Photo 37: Reversed-leg scissors.

Photo 38: Second hip throw.

Photos 39 and 40: Shoulder throw on one knee. Known, according to Van der Bruggen, as the 'Japanese' shoulder throw.

Photo 41: Shoulder wheel.

Photo 42: Group photo at a jiu jitsu demonstration.

The next four photographs show the sparse interior of Nakada, Johan van der Bruggen's school on Zoutmanstraat.

Photo 43: Hip throw with arm lock performed on Hans van der Stok by Johan van der Bruggen, who is wearing plus-fours and standing with at least one shoe on the mat.

Photo 44: Defence against knife attack by means of a shin throw, performed by Van der Bruggen on Hans van der Stok.

Photo 45: Shoulder throw performed by Hans vander Stok.

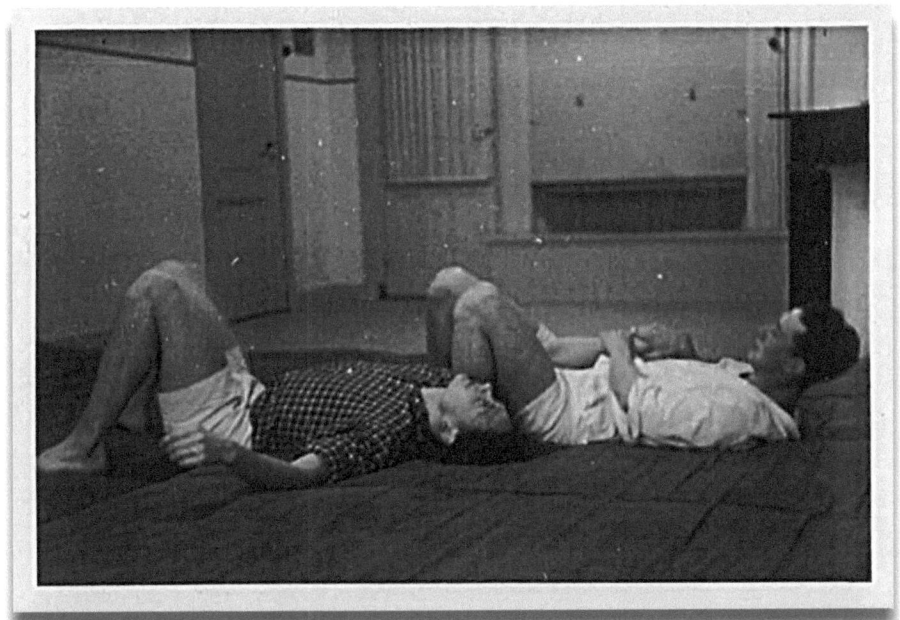

Photo 46: Straight-arm lock performed by Hans van der Stok.

Photo 47: Beginning of a straight-arm lock.

Photo 48: Unidentified technique.

Photo 49: Throw using hand pressure on both knees from behind. The attack consisted of a 'grab around' the arms from behind. It is important for the person being thrown to keep his or her arms straight and to bend the arms and start to roll only once the hands have touched the ground. The two figures in the background show the first phase of a shoulder throw.

Photo 50: The defender pulls back the assailant's arm as he attempts to roll out of the defender's arm lock.

Photo 51: Rolling out of an arm lock in an attempt to escape.

It is possible that photos 49, 50 and 51 are part of a series. Photos 50 and 51 may have been reversed.

Photo 49 shows a defence executed by pushing the knees against a grabbing attack around the arms from behind. It is possible that photo 51 shows how the defender steps forward immediately after throwing his assailant and grabs the attacker's arm while his opponent is still trying to roll out of his fall.

Photo 50 would thus show the defender changing direction and pulling the attacker backwards to secure an arm lock.

Photo 52: Chin throw executed by Hans van der Stok.

Here too, the photos may have been reversed. Photos 50, 51 and 52.

Photo 52 shows a chin throw being employed against an attack from the front. The attack might have been a grab, strike or punch to the face. The technique in photo 50 is likely a follow up to a chin-throw.

If the opponent is not sufficiently unbalanced by the chin throw, the opponent's hand may be placed on the ground far to the rear to make sure he or she is felled.

Assuming that this is the scenario in this series, photo 51 shows the opponent rolling backwards in an attempt to escape.

Photos 53 and 54: The interior of Studio Pulchri during a demonstration.

Photo 55: A diving forward roll over at least seven men – no mean feat.
Van der Bruggen, who is last in the line, seems to be taking no chances:
he has lowered his position slightly.

Photo 56: Van der Bruggen explains a detail to the audience.

Photo 57: Sideways stomach throw by Hans van der Stok.

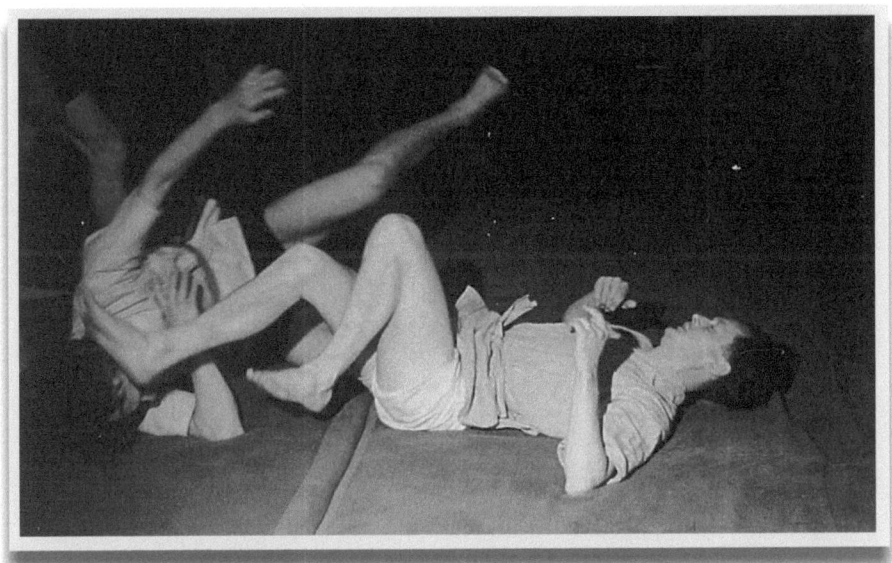

Photo 58: Probably an escape from a strangling attack while on the ground by kicking the assailant away.

Photo 59: Transition from (most likely) a shoulder throw to ground work.

Photo 60: Van der Bruggen and partner demonstrate the basic judo hold and starting position. Van der Bruggen was the first judo instructor in the Netherlands, teaching the sport well before WW2, first in Rotterdam and later in The Hague.

Photo 61: Jiu jitsu ground work.

Photo 62: Jiu jitsu ground work. A wrist lock is used as a submission technique.

Photo 63: Shoulder throw as defence against a strangle with both hands from the side.

Photo 64: A throw by means of pushing the knees as defence against an attack from behind. In this instance the assailant is thrown more diagonally than he should have been.

JIU JITSU

GESLAAGDE DEMONSTRATIE

In zijn school „Nakada" heeft dr. Joh. v. d. Bruggen een zeer interessante demonstratie met leerlingen gegeven van de aantrekkelijke en nuttige zelfverdedigingssport jiu-jitsu, gevolgd door een demonstratie judo, een wedstrijdsport, welke door den instructeur hier te lande is geïntroduceerd en in een goed jaar veel opgang heeft gemaakt.

De demonstratie droeg een heel ander karakter, dan we tot dusverre gewend waren en het moet gezegd worden, dat de nieuwe onderwijsmethode van den heer v. d. Bruggen als een werkelijke vooruitgang moet worden beschouwd. Zeer veel aandacht wordt nu geschonken aan de voorbereidende stof der zelfverdedigingssport en dat is van groote practische beteekenis, vooral wanneer men zich te verdedigen heeft tegen de niets ontziende manieren van straatvechters.

Haagsche Courant
8 Dec. 1941.

Jiu jitsu

Successful demonstration

At his 'Nakada' school, Mr Johan van der Bruggen and his pupils gave a fascinating demonstration of the attractive and useful self-defence sport jiu jitsu. Mr Van der Bruggen then demonstrated the sport of judo, which he introduced into this country and which has seen a significant rise in popularity in little more than a year.

The demonstration was very different in nature to anything we have seen previously and it must be said that Mr Van der Bruggen's new teaching method should be considered a genuine step forward.

A great deal of attention is now paid to the theory and basics of the sport of self-defence. This is important, especially when one is forced to defend oneself against the unscrupulous tactics employed by street fighters.

Haagsche Courant
8 December 1941

De Zachte Kunst

(Door Sportman)

Of het Biggers' fameuze Charley Chan of een andere detective uit het Verre Oosten was, wil ons niet meer te binnen schieten, doch wij herinneren ons van films, die lang geleden draaiden, nog altijd met veel genoegen een oogenschijnlijk weinig forschen speurder, die zijn vaak veel grootere en sterkere aanvallers met zichtbaar gemak en dank zij een enkele mysterieuze kunstgreep baas bleef. Onze in de laatste acte nooit falende jager op misdadigers bleek, behalve op ander terrein, een meester in het jiu jitsu, de Japansche kunst van zelfverdediging. De oorsprong van deze vechtmethode ligt in het duister van lang vervlogen eeuwen verborgen, doch zeker schijnt wel, dat de bewoners van het eilandenrijk in het Verre Oosten haar aan hun buren, de Chineezen, te danken hebben, al hebben de Japanners er later dan ook zeer veel aan toegevoegd. Oorspronkelijk was het systeem geheim, en de adel — t.w. de zoogen. „samurai" — had er het monopolie van. In dien Japansch-Middeleeuwschen tijd was het alleen aan de edelen toegestaan het zwaard te dragen, maar wanneer zij ongewapend tegen tegenstanders van lageren rang en stand in het strijdperk traden, bezaten zij in het jiu jitsu altijd nog een middel om hun superioriteit metterdaad te bewijzen. Later evenwel is deze wijze van vechten, met inbegrip van de eraan verbonden omvangrijke training, in Japan gemeengoed geworden, en thans wordt zij niet alleen aan beide seksen op allerlei onderwijsinrichtingen onderwezen, doch zij vormt er bovendien den grondslag van de lichamelijke oefening. Het duurde tot het begin van deze eeuw, eer het jiu jitsu naar de Oude Wereld werd overgebracht.

Jiu jitsu wordt ook wel „de zachte kunst" genoemd, omdat men niet de bedoeling heeft zijn tegenstander te verwonden óf, in een geval van ernstig handgemeen, om het leven te brengen, doch hem slechts tijdelijk buiten gevecht stelt. Van wapens is geen sprake, en evenmin van de beantwoording van kracht met kracht. Lichaamskracht speelt zelfs een ondergeschikte rol; hoofdzaak zijn een groote handigheid en de anatomische kennis van het menschelijk lichaam waar het geldt er kwetsbare — beter gezegd gevoelige — plaatsen van te ontdekken, en zich die ten nutte te maken. Het komt er op aan den aanvaller juist op die plekken te treffen, en door het toepassen van bepaalde grepen, of een combinatie er van, hem of te verdooven, of te dwingen, zijn verzet te staken. Zou hij bij zijn positieven blijven, en den strijd toch willen voortzetten, dan zou hem dat op een ontwrichten schouder, een gebroken pols of misschien nog erger komen te staan. Onze body vertoont tal van plaatsen, waarop de oogenschijnlijk tengerder Japanner zijn aanval kan concentreeren. Denkt u maar aan uw gevoeligen elleboogsknokkel, aan uw polsen, aan uw nek en aan uw keel! Een greep, een stevige druk of een slag met den kant van een hand (vuistslagen zijn in jiu jitsu niet geoorloofd) op een van deze, of nog vele andere plaatsen, en u bent al goeddeels buiten gevecht gesteld. In jiu-do, de wedstrijdsport die op het Japansche vechten gebaseerd is, zijn natuurlijk tal van middelen, waarnaar men tegenover een inbreker waarschijnlijk wèl zou grijpen, verboden. In dit geval ook zijn de tegenstanders, evenals bij het boksen, in gewichtklassen ingedeeld. Zoodra een tegenstander weet, buiten gevecht te zijn gesteld, klopt hij op den grond, ten einde erger te voorkomen.

59

6 December 1941

The Soft Art
By Sportsman

Whether it was Bigger's famous Charley (sic) Chan, or another
famous detective from the Far East, we do not recall. We do however
remember with affection those movies in which the slender detective
would effortlessly subdue his often bigger and stronger opponents
thanks to his command of a few mysterious techniques. The hunter,
who always got his man in the final act, turned out to be a master of
the Japanese art of jiu jitsu.

The origins of this art form remain obscure, but it seems
certain that though the inhabitants the Far Eastern empire added
much to the art themselves, they first learned the discipline from their
neighbours the Chinese.

Originally the system was a secret, the exclusive preserve of
samurai noblemen. In the Japanese Middle Ages only members of
the nobility were permitted to carry swords. If they ever had to fight
lower-ranking opponents in unarmed combat, they could always
prove their superiority with a display of skill in jiu jitsu.

Later, however, the art form became accessible to all. It is not
only taught to members of both sexes and at all kinds of educational
establishments, but it also now forms the basis for all forms of
physical education. It took until the turn of the century before jiu
jitsu was brought to the Old World.

Jiu jitsu is also called 'the soft art' because the practitioner does not
intend to harm his opponent (or, in the event of a particularly violent
encounter, at least does not intend to kill him), but to render him
temporarily helpless. No weapons are used at all, nor is force ever
met with force. In fact, physical strength is less important than agility,
speed and an understanding of anatomy as it relates to identifying –
and exploiting – the human body's weak spots.

The secret is to strike at these spots to render one's assailant
helpless, to use a given technique or combination of techniques to
make him give up all resistance. If he still puts up a fight, he might

get a dislocated shoulder, a broken wrist, or worse for his trouble.

The Japanese assailant may appear slender at first glance, but our bodies have plenty of weak spots in which he might concentrate his attack. Take your funny bone, and the vulnerable spots on your wrists, your neck and your throat! A grip, a hard push or a strike with the edge of the hand (striking with the fists is prohibited) in any one of these and countless other weak areas would put you out of commission. In jiu-do, the tournament sport based on Japanese combat, many tactics you might employ against a burglar are not permitted.

As in boxing, opponents are divided in weight categories. As soon as an opponent knows he is beaten, he taps the ground to end the bout.

De Rotterdamsch school organiseerde in den loop der jaren uitstekend verzorgde demonstraties van beide takken van sport en kreeg daardoor mede een uitstekenden naam. Vele Rotterdammers zullen zich nog de druk bezochte avonden herinneren. Jammer genoeg leed de jonge Judo-vechter, de heer Van Bruggen, een gevoelig verlies door den oorlog in 1940, toen zijn school geheel afbrandde. Na vele teleurstellingen en met groote moeite heeft hij in 1941 een nieuwe school in Den Haag opgericht.

Velen hebben sindsdien kennis gemaakt met het werk van deze school. Het Jiu-Jitsu en het Judo, op de juiste wijze onderwezen, breekt steeds meer in ons land baan!

(Ingezonden Mededeelingen.)

Over the years the Rotterdam school has performed many demonstrations of both arts and as a result has built an impressive reputation.

Many Rotterdammers will remember these well-attended evenings. Sadly the proprietor, young judo master Mr Van der Bruggen, suffered a great loss when his school burned down in the war in 1940.

With great difficulty and after many set-backs, he founded a new school in The Hague in 1941. Since then, many people have been introduced to the work of the school. Jiu jitsu and judo taught in the correct manner is making more and more headway in our country!

(Letter to the editor)

SCHERMEN
Judo
Interessante demonstraties door den jiu-jitsuleeraar J. v. d. Bruggen

In de schermzaal van Vandervoodt te Rotterdam heeft Zondagmiddag de jiu-jitsuleeraar J. v. d. Bruggen onder groote belangstelling demonstraties gegeven in het jiu-jitsu en het judo. Daarbij waren een achttal gevorderde leerlingen hem behulpzaam Nadat eerst een groot aantal jiu-jitsu-demonstraties waren gegeven, voerden de leerlingen eenige judo-spelen uit. De kunst is daarbij den tegenstander uit het evenwicht te brengen en hem vervolgens door een jiu-jitsu-greep te „vloeren". Het spreekt vanzelf, dat aan dit spel regels verbonden zijn, die een willekeurige beoefening van de grepen verbieden. Er zijn nu eenmaal in jiu-jitsu grepen, die zeer gevaarlijk kunnen zijn. Karakteristiek voor judo is de Japansche groet, die het spel opent.

Uit deze demonstraties, die door het publiek met veel belangstelling werden gevolgd, is wel gebleken, dat judo in de toekomst een belangrijke plaats in de sport kan gaan innemen. Men kan judo-wedstrijden in de naaste toekomst evenwel nog niet tegemoetzien, omdat er nog steeds te weinig beoefenaars dezer spelen zijn, een euvel dat in den loop van den tijd steeds kleiner zal worden, omdat het aantal jiu-jitsu'ers zich gestadig uitbreidt.

Dagblad van Rotterdam
23Dec. 1941

Judo

Interesting demonstration by jiu jitsu instructor J. v.d. Bruggen

At Rotterdam's Vandervoodt fencing school last Sunday,
J. v.d. Bruggen gave demonstrations in the arts of jiu jitsu and judo
that attracted much interest. He was assisted by eight advanced
students.

 Following numerous demonstrations of jiu jitsu the students
performed several judo matches. The art of judo is to upset the
opponent's balance and throw him to the ground using jiu jitsu
techniques. Naturally there are rules which prohibit the use of many
techniques, some of which can be very dangerous.

 A characteristic feature of judo is the Japanese method of
greeting one's opponent at the start of a match.

 It is clear from the level of interest these demonstra-tions
attracted that judo could become a highly popular sport in the future.
But it will be a while before it is possible to organise judo
tournaments since there are currently too few students. With the
steadily rising number of jiu jitsu practitioners, however, this should
not be a problem for long.

Dagblad van Rotterdam
23 December 1941

Boven. Het begin van den Japanschen schouderworp.

Above. Beginning of Japanese shoulder throw

De Japansche schouderworp in volle actie, geheel uitgevoerd volgens de regelen der kunst.

foto's I. P. en R. S.

DE PRINS—HET LEVEN   *7 Febr. 1942.*

Japanese shoulder throw in full swing, executed according to the rules of the art.

Double stomach throw at full speed. This throw requires great agility and self-control.

JIU-JITSU en JUDO

Jiu-Jitsu, de Japansche zelfverdediging, heeft vele aanhangers in Nederland verkregen. Het is daarom niet te verwonderen, dat de tegenwoordige Nederlandsche Jiu-Jitsu Bond zich veel moeite getroost om de sport in rechte banen te leiden. Voorheen waren er immers zeer veel leeraren, die deze sport gedeeltelijk of in het geheel niet kenden. Vaak werd de sport op verkeerde wijze gepropageerd, maar dank zij de N. J. J. B. werd hieraan een einde gemaakt. Een van Nederlands op den voorgrond tredende medewerkers van dien Bond is de heer Johan van der Bruggen, die in 1935 in Indië op de Japansche school van Taiji Nakada het leeraarsdiploma behaalde. Na in Indië aan vele Judo-wedstrijden te hebben deelgenomen, kwam hij in Holland en opende in 1938 zijn school in Rotterdam.

De heer Van Bruggen bracht in Nederland de geheel onbekende Judosport. De Judo-vechter moet buitengewoon veel geduld en zelfbeheersching bezitten. De wedstrijdregels zijn zwaar. Wordt bij Jiu-Jitsu weinig kracht vereischt, het Judo vergt meer. Ondanks dat is deze sport, wat de beginselen betreft, zeer nuttig voor dames en kinderen. Immers dames behouden hun gratie en lenigheid bij het beoefenen van deze sport, terwijl het bij kinderen reeds jong gehoorzaamheid, voorzichtigheid en moed aankweekt. Behalve deze opvoedkundige waarde geeft het Jiu-Jitsu en Judo hun een lichamelijken voorsprong boven anderen.

JIU JITSU AND JUDO

Jiu jitsu, the Japanese art of self-defence has attracted many adherents in the Netherlands. So it is no wonder that the Nederlandse Jiu Jitsu Bond is working hard to steer the sport in the right direction.

Until recently, many instructors were only partly schooled in the art, while others were completely untrained. Often it was taught in the wrong way entirely. But that has changed thanks to the Nederlandse Jiu Jitsu Bond. One of the its foremost teachers is Johan van der Bruggen, who obtained his instructor's license in the Dutch East Indies at the school of Japanese master Taiji Nakada. Having entered many tournaments in the Dutch East Indies, Mr Van der Bruggen came to the Netherlands and opened his school in Rotterdam in 1938.

Mr Van der Bruggen also introduced the art of judo to the Netherlands, a sport previously unknown in this country.

The judo fighter must have extraordinary patience and self-control. The rules of the sport are very tough indeed.

Whereas little strength is required in the practice of jiu jitsu, judo is more demanding. Nevertheless, in principle it is well suited to women and children. With practice, ladies can develop poise and suppleness, while children are encouraged to develop caution, courage and obedience at an early age. Besides these benefits, the two sports also give children a head start in their physical development.

Boven. De Nederl. Jiu-Jitsu Bond beijvert zich om de sport der Japansche zelfverdediging hier te lande in goede banen te leiden. „De omgekeerde schaar" zooals deze wordt onderwezen in de Haagsche school

Above: The Nederlandse Jiu Jitsu Bond is doing its best to ensure that the Japanese art of self-defence is taught the correct way here. The 'reversed scissors', as taught in the 'Hague School'.

Assistant at jiu jitsu demonstration at Metropole Palace on Sunday 29 March (year omitted). Hans van der Stok. (signed, Van der Bruggen)

68

JIU-JITSU
DAMES TOONDEN HAAR BEDREVENHEID,

In den foyer van Metropole Palace werd Zondag een Jiu-Jitsu en Judo-demonstratiemiddag georganiseerd. Het was er zoo vol, dat er schier geen mannetje meer bij kon. Onder de deskundige leiding van den heer Johan van der Bruggen werden hier jong en oud onderricht in de zelfverdediging. Ongeveer anderhalf uur lang hebben we hier lieden van beiderlei kunne over — gelukkig goed gevulde — matrassen zien duikelen. Want dat was het bijzondere, dat wij ook dames in den meest letterlijken zin hebben zien vechten. En dit moet te harer eere worden gezegd, in het toepassen van, op het oog, geniepige kunstgrepen, deden zij voor de mannenbroeders niet onder. De haarspelden hebben voorgoed afgedaan. Een Haagsche schoone zal in den vervolge, bij een eventueelen twist, die in handgemeen ontaardt, naar de regelen van de kunst, bijv. de „schaargreep" toepassen, of wat afdoende is, den aanrander met het been een flinke por in de buik toedienen en zoo noodig door hardhandige omhelzing den adem benemen. Wie deze demonstratie heeft aanschouwd, zal nimmer meer spreken van het „zwakke geslacht". Er waren heel wat oma's onder het aandachtig publiek, dat met zichtbaar welbehagen al deze pogingen tot moord (met voorbedachten rade) gadesloeg. Wellicht zullen zij tot de conclusie zijn gekomen, dat zij in haar jeugd heel wat tekort zijn gekomen. Hulde aan haar nazaten, die, hoe lieftallig van uiterlijk ook, toonden — als het moet — ware Kenau's te zijn. De heer van der Bruggen kan trotsch zijn op zijn leerlingen; hij verdient een compliment voor zijn technische uiteenzetting, welke ons heeft bewogen, tal van grepen in den familiekring te gaan toepassen, al dan niet met goed gevolg.

Jiu jitsu

Ladies show their skills

Last Sunday a demonstration of jiu jitsu and judo was held in the foyer of the Metropole Palace with a huge crowd in attendance. Under the expert guidance of Mr Johan van der Bruggen, young and old alike were introduced to the art of self-defence. For around ninety minutes, we witnessed enthusiasts – male and female – tumbling on to mattresses which fortunately were thick enough to break their falls. Most remarkable of all was the sight of ladies fighting in the most literal sense of the word. And it must be said that in demonstrating their ruthless techniques, they certainly gave as good as the men. Hairpins are gone for good! In future, when an argument turns ugly some Hague beauty will use the 'scissor grip' or give her opponent a well-deserved kick, followed if necessary by a suffocating bear hug. Anyone who witnessed this demonstration will think twice in the future before speaking of a 'weaker sex'.

The appreciative spectators included plenty of grandmothers watching these (pre-meditated!) attempts at murder with great pleasure. Many of them must have concluded that they truly missed out when they were young. We salute their descendents who, lovely as they are, have proven that they can be real battle axes when the occasion demands.

Mr Van der Bruggen can be justly proud of his pupils. He is to be commended for his expert explanation of the techniques involved. He has inspired us to try them out for ourselves at home, though whether we succeed remains to be seen!

A note at the front of the album suggests that it was given to Hans, or that Hans started compiling the album, in August 1940.

It seems unlikely that Hans took the album with him when he left for England in 1942.
After the war, his mother presented it to his teacher, Johan van der Bruggen, as a memento.

It thus seems reasonable to conclude that Hans compiled the album between 1940 and 1942 and that he left it with his mother for safekeeping, possibly planning to retrieve it and continue working on it when his circumstances improved.

Notes

1 – Henk Deinum C.E. (1915 – 1992) was a resistance fighter during the Second World War.

2 – Pierre Louis baron d'Aulnis de Bourouill (b. 1918) was a Dutch resistance fighter during the Second World War.

3 – Fiat Libertas was a nationwide support organisation for stranded pilots in occupied Holland during the Second World War.

4 – De Raad van Verzet (The Council of Resistance) was a Dutch umbrella organisation of resistance groups during the Second World War.

5 – De Ordedienst, was a resistance group consisting mainly of members of the former Dutch army, who wanted to live up to their oath always to remain true to and fight for their fatherland.

6 – Zendgroep Barbara was a group made up of secret agents from the Bureau Inlichtingen. They were trained in radio-telegraphy, code-breaking and encryption.

7 – The Groep Packard (Packard Group) was a Dutch intelligence group during the Second World War.
Its aim was to provide the Allies and the Dutch government in London with military and other intelligence from occupied Holland.

Acknowledgements

My thanks go to the following people:

First and foremost, my friend and colleague Adriaan M. Daleboudt, for his invaluable assistance in preparing the album for publication. Without his help this book simply would not have been possible. Adriaan designed the cover and layout and commented on early drafts. His professionalism and expertise are greatly appreciated.

Elmer van der Kamp, who edited the Dutch edition, and Matthew Tate, who edited the English edition.

F. Buhrmann, for the many times he welcomed me into his home and for his permission to use his family archive.

E.J.J.F. Rossmeisl of the Netherlands Institute of Military History (NIMH), for the information he provided on Hans van der Stok.

R. van Heiningen of the Netherlands Institute for War Documentation (NIOD) for the photograph of Hans van der Stok as a cadet.

B. Grisnigt for the interviews he granted me.

M.H. Breibarth-van der Stok for the portrait of Hans van der Stok.

Bibliography

De bezetter bespied, de Nederlandse Geheime Inlichtingendienst in de Tweede Wereldoorlog (Spying on the Invader: the Dutch Secret Intelligence Service in the Second World War)
Frank Visser
Uitgeverij Thieme, Zutphen, 1983.

Jiujitsu en judo (Jiu Jitsu and Judo)
Maurice van Nieuwenhuizen
A.W. Bruna & zoon's uitgevers-mij. N.V.
Utrecht, 1941.

Nakada: een Haagse jiu-jitsu en judoschool in woord en beeld (Nakada: an illustrated history of the Jiu Jitsu and Judo Academy in The Hague)
J.H.G. Smits
Uitgeverij Boekenplan, 2011
ISBN 978-90-86662067

De Koninklijke Marine in de Tweede Wereldoorlog (The Royal Dutch Navy in the Second World War), *Volume One*
P.M. Bosscher
De Franeker, 1984 -1990

Abridged collection, archive of the Bureau Inlichtingen.

Archive of the Bureau Inlichtingen, Nationaal Archief, The Hague.

Family archive and photo albums of F. Buhrmann, Voorburg.

The author's collection.

Photo archive of the NIOD's Honour Roll of the Fallen, 1940-1945.

About the author

Johan Smits (b. 1961) studied at the Academy for Library and Documentation Studies in The Hague.

He works for the Dutch Ministry of Foreign Affairs and is a practitioner and licensed teacher of jiu jitsu (4th degree black belt).

His interests include researching the history of jiu jitsu in the Netherlands. His previous book examined the history of Nakada, Johan van der Bruggen's sport school in The Hague.